Kessinger Publishing's Rare Reprints

Thousands of Scarce and Hard-to-Find Books on These and other Subjects!

- Americana
- Ancient Mysteries
- Animals
- Anthropology
- Architecture
- Arts
- Astrology
- Bibliographies
- Biographies & Memoirs
- Body, Mind & Spirit
- Business & Investing
- Children & Young Adult
- Collectibles
- Comparative Religions
- Crafts & Hobbies
- Earth Sciences
- Education
- Ephemera
- Fiction
- Folklore
- Geography
- Health & Diet
- History
- Hobbies & Leisure
- Humor
- Illustrated Books
- Language & Culture
- Law
- Life Sciences
- Literature
- Medicine & Pharmacy
- Metaphysical
- Music
- Mystery & Crime
- Mythology
- Natural History
- Outdoor & Nature
- Philosophy
- Poetry
- Political Science
- Science
- Psychiatry & Psychology
- Reference
- Religion & Spiritualism
- Rhetoric
- Sacred Books
- Science Fiction
- Science & Technology
- Self-Help
- Social Sciences
- Symbolism
- Theatre & Drama
- Theology
- Travel & Explorations
- War & Military
- Women
- Yoga
- *Plus Much More!*

We kindly invite you to view our catalog list at:
http://www.kessinger.net

OLD TESTAMENT APOCRYPHA

THE GREEK APOCALYPSE OF BARUCH

"*And the angel of the powers said to me, Come and I will show thee the mysteries of God.*"

—BARUCH.

THE GREEK APOCALYPSE OF BARUCH

(INTRODUCTION)

THERE is a Book of Baruch among those apocrypha which our general introduction described as of the first class; that is, books still accepted by the Roman Catholic church and occasionally reprinted even in Protestant Bibles. There are also six or seven other Baruch apocrypha. Baruch's name was naturally borrowed as one under which to announce religious preachings; for he appears in the Old Testament as a lesser prophet or scribe, the staunch supporter of the greater prophet Jeremiah through all the latter's tribulations. Again and again Baruch is represented as reading to the people from his book. Hence many books were afterward assigned to him.

Among these was the Apocalypse here given. It is a Greek work of the second century after Christ; but behind this there must have been a Jewish original, for much of the thought is Hebraic. This Greek version was written by a Christian, whose main purpose seems to have been to warn the unconverted Jews of their wickedness in not accepting Christianity. This then is a typical apocrypha of the " apocalypse " class. That is, it depicts an ancient prophet as foreseeing the end of the world, or in this case the heavens beyond the world, and it describes this vision with an earnest ethical purpose.

The " seven heavens " described in this apocalypse form the most complete and fully organized idea of a heavenly kingdom or social world preserved from Hebraic or early Christian teaching. Indeed it is the theology of this book which lends its chief interest. The intercession of angels for men is taught, and, more important still, Adam is not represented as plunging all his race into sin. Each man is here definitely declared to be his own Adam, causing his own fall. " The men who now drink insatiably the wine . . . transgress worse than Adam."

THE APOCALYPSE OF BARUCH

CHAPTER I — PROLOGUE

A narrative and revelation of Baruch, concerning those ineffable things which he saw by command of God. Bless Thou, O Lord.

A revelation of Baruch, who stood upon the river Gel weeping over the captivity of Jerusalem, when also Abimelech [1] was preserved by the hand of God, at the farm of Agrippa. [2] And he was sitting thus at the beautiful gates, where the Holy of holies lay.

Verily I, Baruch, was weeping in my mind and sorrowing on account of the people, and that Nebuchadrezzar the King was permitted by God to destroy His city, saying: Lord, why didst Thou set on fire Thy vineyard, and lay it waste? Why didst Thou do this? And why, Lord, didst Thou not requite us with another chastisement, but didst deliver us to nations such as these, so that they reproach us and say, Where is their God? And behold as I was weeping and saying such things, I saw an angel of the Lord coming and saying to me: Understand, O man, greatly beloved, and trouble not thyself so greatly concerning the salvation of Jerusalem, for thus saith the Lord God the Almighty. For He sent me before thee, to make known and to show to thee all the things of God. For thy prayer was heard before Him, and entered into the ears of the Lord God. And when

---

[1] It is recorded that Abimelech fell asleep in the garden of Agrippa at the time of the destruction of Jerusalem, and did not awake for sixty-six years.

[2] "The farm of Agrippa." Rendel Harris identifies this with the fertile valley below Solomon's Pools, known as Solomon's Gardens. See Josephus, "Antiquities," viii. 7. 3, "There was a certain place about fifty furlongs distant from Jerusalem, which is called Etham, very pleasant it is in fine gardens, and abounding in rivulets of water; thither did he (Solomon) use to go out in the morning."

he had said these things to me, I was silent. And the angel said to me: Cease to provoke God, and I will show thee other mysteries, greater than these. And I, Baruch, said, As the Lord God liveth, if thou wilt show me, and I hear a word of thine, I will not continue to speak any longer. God shall add to my judgment in the day of judgment, if I speak hereafter. And the angel of the powers said to me, Come and I will show thee the mysteries of God.

CHAPTER II — THE FIRST HEAVEN

And he took me and led me where the firmament has been set fast, and where there was a river which no one can cross, nor any strange breeze of all those which God created. And he took me and led me to the first heaven, and showed me a door of great size. And he said to me, Let us enter through it, and we entered as though borne on wings, a distance of about thirty days' journey. And he showed me within the heaven a plain; and there were men dwelling thereon, with the faces of oxen, and the horns of stags, and the feet of goats, and the haunches of lambs. And I, Baruch, asked the angel, Make known to me, I pray thee, what is the thickness of the heaven in which we journeyed, or what is its extent, or what is the plain, in order that I may also tell the sons of men? And the angel whose name is Phamael said to me: This door which thou seest is the door of heaven, and as great as is the distance from earth to heaven, so great also is its thickness; and again as great as is the distance from North to South, so great is the length of the plain which thou didst see. And again the angel of the powers said to me, Come, and I will show thee greater mysteries. But I said, pray thee show me what are these men. And he said to me, These are they who built the tower of strife against God, and the Lord banished them.

CHAPTER III — THE SECOND HEAVEN

And the angel of the Lord took me and led me to a second heaven. And he showed me there also a door like the first and said, Let us enter through it. And we entered, being

borne on wings a distance of about sixty days' journey.
And he showed me there also a plain, and it was full of men,
whose appearance was like that of dogs, and whose feet were
like those of stags. And I asked the angel: I pray thee,
Lord, say to me who are these. And he said, These are they
who gave counsel to build the tower, for they whom thou
seest drove forth multitudes of both men and women, to
make bricks; among whom, a woman making bricks was
not allowed to be released in the hour of child-birth, but
brought forth while she was making bricks, and carried her
child in her apron, and continued to make bricks. And the
Lord appeared to them and confused their speech, when they
had built the tower to the height of four hundred and sixty-
three cubits. And they took a gimlet, and sought to pierce
the heaven, saying, Let us see whether the heaven is made
of clay, or of brass, or of iron. When God saw this He did
not permit them, but smote them with blindness and confusion of speech, and rendered them as thou seest.

CHAPTER IV — THE THIRD HEAVEN

And I, Baruch, said, Behold, Lord, Thou didst show me
great and wonderful things; and now show me all things for
the sake of the Lord. And the angel said to me, Come, let
us proceed. And I proceeded with the angel from that place
about one hundred and eighty-five days' journey. And he
showed me a plain and a serpent, which appeared to be two
hundred plethra in length. And he showed me Hades, and
its appearance was dark and abominable. And I said, Who
is this dragon, and who is this monster around him? And
the angel said, The dragon is he who eats the bodies of those
who spend their life wickedly, and he is nourished by them.
And this is Hades, which itself also closely resembles him,
in that it also drinks about a cubit from the sea, which does
not sink at all. Baruch said, And how does this happen?
And the angel said, Harken, the Lord God made three hundred and sixty rivers, of which the chief of all are Alphias,
Abyrus, and the Gericus; and because of these the sea does
not sink. And I said, I pray thee show me which is the

tree which led Adam astray.[3]   And the angel said to me, It is the vine,[4] which the angel Sammael [5] planted, whereat the Lord God was angry, and He cursed him and his plant, while also on this account He did not permit Adam to touch it, and therefore the devil being envious deceived him through his vine.   [And I, Baruch, said,[6] Since also the vine has been the cause of such great evil, and is under judgment of the curse of God, and was the destruction of the first created, how is it now so useful?   And the angel said, Thou askest aright.   When God caused the deluge upon earth, and destroyed all flesh, and four hundred and nine thousand giants, and the water rose fifteen cubits above the highest mountains, then the water entered into paradise and destroyed every flower; but it removed wholly without the bounds the shoot of the vine and cast it outside.   And when the earth appeared out of the water, and Noah came out of the ark, he began to plant of the plants which he found.   But he found also the shoot of the vine; and he took it, and was reasoning in himself, What then is it?   And I came and spake to him the things concerning it.   And he said, Shall I plant it, or what shall I do?   Since Adam was destroyed because of it, let me not also meet with the anger of God because of it.   And saying these things he prayed that God would reveal to him what he should do concerning it.   And

[3] " The tree which led Adam astray."   The transition is sudden, but there may be a hiatus in the narrative. Baruch is still in the third heaven, where paradise was placed, and by now the angel may have shown him it.   In the Slavonic the story of the vine does not break into the description of the dragon, but comes after it.

[4] The conception of the grape-vine as the forbidden tree is very old. It is related of Shamdon (Asmodeus) that at the planting of the first vine by Noah, he helped with the work and said to Noah: " I want to join you in your labor and share with you; but take heed that I take not of your portion, lest I do you harm." The story does not occur elsewhere in the exact form of that of the text.

[5] Slavonic reads " Satanïl."   Sammael was originally one of the chief archangels, but tempted Eve with a view to making the earth his kingdom.   Thenceforth he is the chief of the Satans, the angel of death, and Israel's special foe.

[6] The passage in brackets is clearly an interpolation by the Christian redactor, who felt it necessary to modify the condemnation of wine, on account of its use in the Eucharist.

when hɔ had completed the prayer which lasted forty days, and having besought many things and wept, he said: Lord, I entreat thee to reveal to me what I shall do concerning this plant. But God sent his angel Sarasael, and said to him, Arise, Noah, and plant the shoot of the vine, for thus saith the Lord: Its bitterness shall be changed into sweetness, and its curse shall become a blessing, and that which is produced from it shall become the blood of God; and as through it the human race obtained condemnation, so again through Jesus Christ the Immanuel will they receive in Him the upward calling, and the entry into paradise.] Know therefore, O Baruch, that as Adam through this very tree obtained condemnation, and was divested of the glory of God, so also the men who now drink insatiably the wine which is begotten of it transgress worse than Adam, and are far from the glory of God, and are surrendering themselves to the eternal fire. For no good comes through it. For those who drink it to surfeit do these things: neither does a brother pity his brother, nor a father his son, nor children their parents, but from the drinking of wine come all evils, such as murders, adulteries, fornications, perjuries, thefts, and such like. And nothing good is established by it.

CHAPTER V

And I, Baruch, said to the angel, Let me ask thee one thing, Lord. Since thou didst say to me that the dragon drinks one cubit out of the sea, say to me also, how great is his belly? And the angel said, His belly is Hades; and as far as a plummet is thrown by three hundred men, so great is his belly. Come, then, that I may show thee also greater works than these.

CHAPTER VI

And he took me and led me where the sun goes forth; and he showed me a chariot and four, under which burnt a fire, and in the chariot was sitting a man, wearing a crown of fire, and the chariot was drawn by forty angels. And behold a bird circling before the sun, about nine cubits away. And

I said to the angel, What is this bird? And he said to me, This is the guardian of the earth. And I said, Lord, how is he the guardian of the earth? Teach me. And the angel said to me, This bird flies alongside of the sun, and, expanding his wings, receives its fiery rays. For if he were not receiving them, the human race would not be preserved, nor any other living creature. But God appointed this bird thereto. And he expanded his wings, and I saw on his right wing very large letters, as large as the space of a threshing-floor, the size of about four thousand modii; and the letters were of gold. And the angel said to me, Read them. And I read, and they ran thus: Neither earth nor heaven bring me forth, but wings of fire bring me forth. And I said, Lord, what is this bird, and what is his name? And the angel said to me, his name is called Phoenix. And I said, And what does he eat? And he said to me, The manna of heaven and the dew of earth. And I said, Does the bird excrete? And he said to me, He excretes a worm, and the excrement of the worm is cinnamon, which kings and princes use. But wait and thou shalt see the glory of God. And while he was conversing with me, there was as a thunder-clap, and the place was shaken on which we were standing. And I asked the angel, My Lord, what is this sound? And the angel said to me, Even now the angels are opening the three hundred and sixty-five gates of heaven, and the light is being separated from the darkness. And a voice came which said, Light-giver, give to the world radiance. And when I heard the noise of the bird, I said, Lord, what is this noise? And he said, This is the bird who awakens from slumber the cocks upon earth.[7] For as men do through the mouth, so also does the cock signify to those in the world, in

---

[7] It is doubtful whether there is not here a confusion between the tradition of the phoenix and that of the heavenly cock. As a sun-bird the Greeks made the cock attend on Helios and Apollo. According to an Armenian tradition the heavenly cock first crows, and the angelic choirs begin their hymns of praise. These are heard by the cock on earth, who then awakens mankind, and himself lauds the Creator. There is a passage in the Vendidad, where Sraosha, the angel who sets the world in motion, is likened to " the bird named Parodas (fore-seer) which ill-

his own speech. For the sun is made ready by the angels, and the cock crows.

CHAPTER VII

And I said, And where does the sun begin its labors after the cock crows? And the angel said to me, Listen, Baruch: All things whatsover I showed thee are in the first and second heaven, and in the third heaven the sun passes through and gives light to the world. But wait, and thou shalt see the glory of God. And while I was conversing with him, I saw the bird, and he appeared in front, and grew less and less, and at length returned to his full size. And behind him I saw the shining sun, and the angels which draw it, and a crown upon its head, the sight of which we were not able to gaze upon, and behold. And as soon as the sun shone, the Phoenix also stretched out his wings. But I, when I beheld such great glory, was brought low with great fear, and I fled and hid in the wings of the angel. And the angel said to me, Fear not, Baruch, but wait and thou shalt also see their setting.

CHAPTER VIII

And he took me and led me toward the west; and when the time of the setting came, I saw again the bird coming before it, and as soon as he came I saw the angels, and they lifted the crown from its head. But the bird stood exhausted and with wings contracted. And beholding these things, I said, Lord, wherefore did they lift the crown from the head of the sun, and wherefore is the bird so exhausted? And the angel said to me, The crown of the sun, when it has run through the day — four angels take it, and bear it up to heaven, and renew it, because it and its rays have been defiled upon earth; moreover it is so renewed each day. And I, Baruch, said, Lord, and wherefore are its beams defiled upon earth? And the angel said to me, Because it

speaking people call Kahrkatas, the bird that lifts up his voice against the holy dawn," and calls men to worship and firelighting, lest Bush-yasta, the long-handed demon of procrastination, come upon them.

beholds the lawlessness and unrighteousness of men, namely fornications, adulteries, thefts, extortions, idolatries, drunkenness, murders, strife, jealousies, evil-speakings, murmurings, whisperings, divinations, and such like, which are not well-pleasing to God. On account of these things is it defiled, and therefore is it renewed. But thou askest concerning the bird, how it is exhausted. Because by restraining the rays of the sun through the fire and burning heat of the whole day, it is exhausted thereby. For, as we said before, unless his wings were screening the rays of the sun, no living creature would be preserved.

CHAPTER IX

And they having retired, the night also fell, and at the same time came the chariot of the moon, along with the stars. And I, Baruch, said, Lord, show me it also, I beseech of thee, how it goes forth, where it departs, and in what form it moves along. And the angel said, Wait and thou shalt see it also shortly. And on the morrow I also saw it in the form of a woman, and sitting on a wheeled chariot. And there were before it oxen and lambs in the chariot, and a multitude of angels in like manner. And I said, Lord, what are the oxen and the lambs? And he said to me, They also are angels. And again I asked, Why is it that it one time increases, but at another time decreases? And he said to me, Listen, O Baruch: This which thou seest had been written by God beautiful as no other. And at the transgression of the first Adam, it was near to Sammael when he took the serpent as a garment. And it did not hide itself but increased, and God was angry with it, and afflicted it, and shortened its days.[8] And I said, And how does it not also shine always, but only in the night? And the angel said, Listen: as in the presence of a king, the courtiers can not speak freely, so the moon and the stars can not shine in

[8] The Slavonic attributes the fall of the moon to the fact that it laughed at the fall of Adam and Eve. R. Simeon ben Pazzi declared that at the time of the creation the moon was of the same size as the sun. The moon then objected that it would not be decorous for two kings to use one crown, whereupon God diminished her size.

the presence of the sun; for the stars are always suspended, but they are screened by the sun, and the moon, although it is uninjured, is consumed by the heat of the sun.

CHAPTER X — THE FOURTH HEAVEN

And when I had learned all these things from the archangel, he took and led me into a fourth heaven. And I saw a monotonous plain, and in the middle of it a pool of water. And there were in it multitudes of birds of all kinds, but not like those here on earth. But I saw a crane as great as great oxen; and all the birds were great beyond those in the world. And I asked the angel, What is the plain, and what the pool, and what the multitudes of birds around it? And the angel said, Listen, Baruch: The plain which contains in it the pool and other wonders is the place where the souls of the righteous come, when they hold converse, living together in choirs. But the water is that which the clouds receive, and rain upon the earth, and the fruits increase. And I said again to the angel of the Lord, But what are these birds? And he said to me, They are those which continually sing praise to the Lord. And I said, Lord, and how do men say that the water which descends in rain is from the sea? [9] And the angel said, The water which descends in rain — this also is from the sea, and from the waters upon earth; but that which stimulates the fruits is only from the latter source. Know therefore henceforth that from this source is what is called the dew of the heaven.

CHAPTER XI — THE FIFTH HEAVEN

And the angel took me and led me thence to a fifth heaven. And the gate was closed. And I said, Lord, is not this gateway open that we may enter? And the angel said to me,

[9] The Slavonic reads: "How do men say that the clouds go out of the sea and rain on the earth? And the angel said to me: The race of man is deceived knowing nothing. All the water of the sea is salt, for if the rain came from the sea, no fruit would grow on the earth." The meaning of the Greek seems to be that while the rain is derived in part from the sea, those elements which are responsible for the dew and for the growth of fruit are derived from the other waters upon earth.

We can not enter until Michael comes, who holds the keys of the Kingdom of Heaven; but wait and thou shalt see the glory of God. And there was a great sound, as thunder. And I said, Lord, what is this sound? And he said to me, Even now Michael, the commander of the angels, comes down to receive the prayers of men. And behold a voice came, Let the gates be opened.[10] And they opened them, and there was a roar as of thunder. And Michael came, and the angel who was with me came face to face with him and said, Hail, my commander, and that of all our order. And the commander Michael said, Hail thou also, our brother, and the interpreter of the revelations to those who pass through life virtuously. And having saluted one another thus, they stood still. And I saw the commander Michael, holding an exceedingly great vessel; its depth was as great as the distance from heaven to earth, and its breadth as great as the distance from north to south. And I said, Lord, what is that which Michael the archangel is holding? And he said to me, This is where the merits of the righteous enter, and such good works as they do, which are escorted before the heavenly God.

CHAPTER XII

And as I was conversing with them, behold angels came bearing baskets full of flowers. And they gave them to Michael. And I asked the angel, Lord, who are these, and what are the things brought hither from beside them? And he said to me, These are angels who are over the righteous. And the archangel took the baskets, and cast them into the vessel. And the angel said to me, These flowers are the merits of the righteous. And I saw other angels bearing baskets which were neither empty nor full. And they began to lament, and did not venture to draw near, because they had not the prizes complete. And Michael cried and said,

[10] The idea that the gates of heaven are opened at a fixed time to receive the prayers of men is found in the fragments of the Apocrypha of Adam, where it is stated that at the tenth hour "the gate of heaven opens in order to let in the prayers of every living thing . . . At this hour all that a man asks of God is granted him."

Come hither, also, ye angels, bring what ye have brought.
And Michael was exceedingly grieved, and the angel who
was with me, because they did not fill the vessel.

CHAPTER XIII

And then came in like manner other angels weeping and
bewailing, and saying with fear, Behold how we are over-
clouded, O Lord, for we were delivered to evil men, and we
wish to depart from them. And Michael said, Ye can not
depart from them, in order that the enemy may not prevail
to the end; but say to me what ye ask. And they said, We
pray thee, Michael our commander transfer us from them,
for we can not abide with wicked and foolish men, for there
is nothing good in them, but every kind of unrighteousness
and greed. For we do not behold them entering [into
Church at all, nor among spiritual fathers, nor][11] into any
good work. But where there is murder, there also are they
in the midst, and where are fornications, adulteries, thefts,
slanders, perjuries, jealousies, drunkenness, strife, envy,
murmurings, whispering, idolatry, divination, and such like,
then are they workers of such works, and of others worse.
Wherefore we entreat that we may depart from them. And
Michael said to the angels, Wait till I learn from the Lord
what shall come to pass.

CHAPTER XIV

And in that very hour Michael departed, and the doors
were closed. And there was a sound as thunder. And I
asked the angel, What is the sound? And he said to me,
Michael is even now presenting the merits of men to God.

CHAPTER XV

And in that very hour Michael descended, and the gate
was opened; and he brought oil. And as for the angels
which brought the baskets which were full, he filled them
with oil, saying, Take it away, reward our friends an hun-
dredfold, and those who have laboriously wrought good

[11] The clause in brackets is a Christian interpolation.

works. For those who sowed virtuously also reap virtuously. And he said also to those bringing the half-empty baskets, Come hither ye also; take away the reward according as ye brought, and deliver it to the sons of men. [Then he said also to those who brought the full and to those who brought the half-empty baskets: Go and bless our friends, and say to them that thus saith the Lord, Ye are faithful over a few things, I will set you over many things; enter into the joy of your Lord.][12]

CHAPTER XVI

And turning he said also to those who brought nothing: Thus saith the Lord, Be not sad of countenance, and weep not, nor let the sons of men alone. But since they angered me in their works, go and make them envious and angry and provoked against a people that is no people, a people that has no understanding. Further, besides these, send forth the caterpillar and the unwinged locust, and the mildew, and the common locust and hail with lightnings and anger, and punish them severely with the sword and with death, and their children with demons. For they did not harken to my voice, nor did they observe my commandments, nor do them, but were despisers of my commandments, and insolent toward the priests who proclaimed my words to them.

CHAPTER XVII

And while he yet spake, the door was closed, and we withdrew. And the angel took me and restored me to the place where I was at the beginning. And having come to myself, I gave glory to God, who counted me worthy of such honor. Wherefore do ye also, brethren, who obtained such a revelation, yourselves also glorify God, so that He also may glorify you, now and ever, and to all eternity. Amen.

[12] The words in brackets are a Christian interpolation, as is evident not only from the quotation from Matthew, but also from the fact that the re-enumeration of the first two classes of angels destroys the symmetry of the passage.

This is the end of this publication.

Any remaining blank pages are for our book binding
requirements and are blank on purpose.

To search thousands of interesting publications like this one,
please remember to visit our website at:

http://www.kessinger.net